All the Ways We Could Have Met

Selected Poems
by Susan Culver

All the Ways We Could Have Met
Selected Poems
© 2005 by Susan Culver
All rights reserved.

No part of this book may be reproduced or transmitted in any form or by any means, graphic, electronic or mechanical, including photocopying or recording, taping or any information storage retrieval system without the written permission of the author.

For information, address:
Lulu.com
3131 RDU Center Dr. Suite 210
Morrisville NC 27560
http://www.lulu.com

ISBN 1-4116-4866-8

Printed in the United States of America

For Amanda, Alexis & Alia.
May your lives be filled with ways.

Contents

One: Collisions and Other Chance Encounters

Collision I-II	11
Union Station	13
Trust	14
Chance Encounter	15
Shotgun	18
The Problem With Old Hustlers and New Hookers	20
El Dorado	21
From a Room in an Unnamed Hotel	22
Learning the Kiss	23
Collision III	24

Two: Longing and Consideration

Longing	27
The River Princess	29
Letters to You in Winter	30
Mourning Midas	31
Past the Cul De Sac	32
Consider	33
Once Green	34
The Arrogance of Two	35
Abell 2218	36
The Last Butterfly	38

Three: Confined By Need

Solitary Confinement	41
What is Effortless	42

No Words for Summer's End	43
Shaped By This Need	44
When Clicking Heels Offer No Escape	47
You First	48
Some Days	49
Alive	50
But She Wrote Anyway	52
I Still Need You	53
Unfinished Symphony	54

Four: Reasons, Meanings

She Whispered to the Moon	57
Lily, You Said	58
What He Did	59
The Greatest Fear	60
Speaking of Today	61
And Then, She Opens Her Eyes	62
Another Autumn	64
Reconciliation	66
You Had Your Reasons	67
The Meaning of This	69
Nearly Home	70

Acknowledgments 71

Part One: Collisions and Other Chance Encounters

Collision

I.

Imagine what we might have been,
what we are in secret,
these neon signs of us,
flashing too far from the city
to be anything
but an unexplainable heat,
a transient blinking,
small twinklings so divine
as to hurt, if only we learn ourselves
enough to know
if they're really there at all.

II.

Listen: there is a story here
that I have been trying to tell you,
it's the one where night blocks the path,
sprays the street with gas,
with broken glass, nonessential pieces
of a metal casket. Inside the wreck,
I am tangled in the wreckage of myself,
wondering who will love the children now,
who will plant kisses in their palms
along with all the quarters,
the syllables, the scattered maps.
Tangled, and you are first on the scene,
emerging as you do in flashes of red and blue,
emerging as you do with the words

I would have surely said if I was real to me,
had ever known my own heart well enough
to write a poem for it. You're telling me
to hold on, to breathe. You are tearing
at this broken cage but the cage won't give
and there are moments in this moment
when I am asking you to save me,
times when I think I can save myself.

There are moments in this moment
when our hands touch, our voices fall
and rise again like a simple song,
shimmering shards of a vessel broken
and then pieced together
to make something better, something more alive
than ever before. There are times
when it doesn't matter, the savior or the saved;
the ways in which we both become
one and the same, fighting as we are
on both sides of this shell.

Union Station

We painted a station on Fifth and Main, on all the corners of my mind. In a room near the rickety tracks, you saw my dreams roll by in their slim silver fury, in their rumbling righteousness.

And you let the smoke of them color the sky, let their industrial scent seep through an open window. You saw me smile at the distant desires drawn on all their outer walls, the way I etched a memory of each in the dust on the sill.

And you watched me weep when they went away, taking the people, the praises and even the seasons. Baby, I begged you to bring back the trains but you brought me here instead, you said I could sing in some new ones.

They were my dreams, after all. You were only watching because I needed you to.

Trust

Morning blooms and fades
in shades of azalea,
beautiful like aftermath is beautiful
in that distant instant
between the slap and the ache,
before the day whittles its way
from welt to bruise
and all that falls is forgotten;

beautiful like aftermath is beautiful

in that distant instant, you
tossing petals off the edge of a dream
and me scrabbling to gather them,
so sure each one meant something
that I stepped off the earthen ledge,
into that deep blue breath between
all the things you never said it meant
and the way I woke up falling.

Chance Encounter

I.

I have been building a memory
we never shared, how you were
a younger man then, far
from any interstate, finding your way
across a landscape just south of heaven

and I haven't worked out all the details,
my reason for being there or yours,
but I was bold enough
to have called to you, strong enough
to shoulder your gaze.

Maybe you never even knocked
on the door and there was never a wall
between us or anything but words
that came as they do, in stops and starts,
a maze of other times, other faces

and you wanted me, thought to stay a while,
but something called you back to the path
that claimed you first. There was a voice
you would remember and it was this:

all I had to give.

II.

Try to recall what season it was
when these mountains so haunted you,
when you began to crave those sharp edges
in shades of green and gold and you

had a dozen things that could never be explained,
the way some days the air felt too heavy,
how you knew the stars - so faded
by your city of lights - were closer

than they seemed, how you followed
the work of an unknown artist
for years and years because she painted
dirt roads overgrown by weeds,

sprinkled with bluebells, wild lilies,
and somehow it made you believe
that a place like this could still exist
out here, somewhere, just beyond your reach.

III.

By the time I reach your sea, I have journeyed with my children, grandchildren, have passed a dozen cities all crying to come along. The water's greeting is something first smelled, something felt, offers its own gentle warning:

One must catch her beautiful breath,
clear a place in memory's cluttered space.

Only here is the city less a stranger, on this shore where the houses loom at my back like sepia photos of lovers who long for the return of the boats.

Relying on the arm of my daughter's daughter, I make my way along the beach, stopping so she can gather shells, pass them to me, still warm from her hands, from the hands of the sun.

We are wondering if there is truth to the tale, that a wave's whisper is caught in each pearly conch. My shy smile cannot mask this want for such things.

The girl's steady hand holds the cup to my ear and I can hear you now, not as a liquid echo but a voice so clear as to almost still my heart, lay me to rest on the sand, you in my granddaughter's hand, speaking more than your words, more than mine, speaking whole languages wrapped in that other time. My body is as young as the girl's, your arms strong around my waist, your face smiling down with secrets I have held inside for sixty years, alive, awakening in me this utter need for truth. Today I tell the story of two moments caught in the pink curl of the shell: the moment we met and this one, played and played again for my ears, now hers, now yours.

Played and played again until that sweet girl lowers me to the ground, covers my shoulders with her sweater, with her arm, until twilight finds me huddled, sepia toned, glowing with an inner light, squinting at the horizon where there is a small spot growing in the distance, a single boat returning. *Oh, how I have longed for you.*

Shotgun

I could have been a waitress
in some flatland city
where the horizon is an unbroken line;
in a place that serves steak and spirits;
where happy hour starts at five and lasts all night.

I could have watched you walk in,
quintessential businessman; a rising star.
Money is no object to you
and you would rather sit at a table than the bar.

We could have made
our acquaintance over the menu,
I could have blushed twice
at the way you caught my eye
with the kind of look
that a woman feels right down to her toes
(but mainly in her stomach);
the kind the other girls whisper about on the side.

You could have called me to your table
a half dozen times.
I could have asked how you liked your meat
(obsessed over the way you said rare).
I could have filled your cup,
hid in a quiet corner
while you were drinking me up in your mind.

I could have memorized the name
on your credit card,

missed a breath on the twenty dollar tip
for a fifteen dollar meal.
I could have watched you saunter out,
slip into a silver car with its top down.

I could have watched you drive away
and even still, the dreams would be the same:
you sailing past those bright city lights
to your home in the sky.
Me with the wind in my hair,
riding shotgun.

The Problem With Old Hustlers and New Hookers

We might find ourselves on the hood of a rusted car,
beneath a hungry desert moon and you
would compare me to the night, tell me
that I'm beautiful and if I heard you,
I would feel obliged to pretend that I understood
the tour you took twelve years before I was born.
You would cry, would cling to me, my drowning sailor,
your tears soaking into my skin,
would say you loved me for listening
until the sun came up, how we should call it even.

We would have slipped our darkness into our pockets
by then, a little Saigon into my womb
and you would sing *Sweet Home Alabama*
all the way back to the city, drop me at the corner
of nation three decades gone and still so desperate.

You wouldn't even know my name.

El Dorado

And if you should find me in the shimmer
of morning, battened down in an early shiver,
I shall slink from beneath my white flag sheets,
uncovered as you draw closer. And if your touches
should advance across the landscape of my skin,
hip to valley to hip again, my pulse will rise up
against you; I will yearn to show you the beauty
of what you take. And if you press into me,
shatter silence with a whisper - *Baby* - the single word
shall win the war one breath at a time,
set all of my borders aflame. I shall be your city of gold.

A Room in an Unnamed Hotel

In this fantasy we are burning
not as flames but beacons,
we are speaking without speaking,
uttering our stories in a dialect
of pulse and breath,
so fevered are we in this raft
of having said but never said enough.

Beyond this paper wall
there is a song of water
spilling from a sink, not of its own
accord but by what I have filled past full
for the sake of holding that
which will not survive outside this room,
to which treasures wait in the space of my heart.

Darling, in this fantasy we are drowning,
dropping through layers of glass
and dust and clouds. We are twin flickers
ticking away those second hand sun rays,
dropping down, unknown to the knowing world,
unseen by anyone, anything beyond ourselves.

Learning the Kiss

And when she kisses him,
his mouth is a crowded classroom,
a lecture that begins with hush,
his liquid history one of lamp posts,
ice cream, all the girls he's ever known,
the secret flavors of them:
cinnamon, syrah, mother's milk;
armies of words, curses uttered
in the presence of men and then again,
things spoken soft as song:
honor, daughter, love;
words she's never heard before,
what he says when he's afraid,
the way he whispers her name
and all the breaths between
the kisses and the speech,
every tattered, shattered sigh,
what he holds in, what sustains him,
what he lets go and barely remembers,
each little death, every morning after,
the laughter and so many lessons of him
she is only beginning to learn.

Collision

III.

Then again, you begin and end
as a warrior and I, a guileless whore,
a saddened queen,
a peasant teen too thirsty
for this first sweet taste of lust.

Today, I am all three of these,
with tears to spill in the cracks of your armor,
cries to haunt your thoughts. I need, I want...

You have brought your gifts to me:
a sky blue feather, a thread of silver,
a stone hot and smooth as a heart.

You wonder if it will be enough to cover the bruises,
to make a dress for me to dance in. You wonder
if it will be enough to draw my hands
to the wall of my chest, to feel the war within,
fighting as I am on both sides of this shell.

I have not fought alone.

Part Two:
Longing and Consideration

Longing

I.

There is something to be said
for small spaces, shells,
for knowing the what's what of this,
that I begin here, end there,
that the span of me fills a room
with no windows, no doors
for you to enter through.

Something to be said, there is,
for loneliness, the wishing well of it,
that I should throw a penny down the shaft of sleep,
never dream to ask for it back, never need
that single moment, love; wasn't born
to spend my life learning to describe it.

II.

Outside there is a world of glass ceilings,
borders, wounds where we touch,
retreat, turn away. There are a million ways
to ache and beyond that: a city of you,
a distance to be erased.

Sometimes I think I hear you calling my name,
that you are the voice that says reach,
reach beyond the golden scrim of things,
the liquid light as far as the eye can see,

as though you are these,
as if I had wings, sometimes.

III.

This is desperation:
That I should have you
and have you not enough,
that there would be so many words
I still couldn't say, but I wanted to.
There is a part of me you cannot press yourself inside,
a place behind your eyes where only you can go.
That the earth should not burn when we kiss,
has no conquered nations to claim, but walls
of us that shall never bear our names,
that we could breathe with or without us.
That all we are, will ever be,
is you.
And me.

IV.

And yet hope remains,
the stain that paints the morning,
slips the heart from its hard, hard wrapping,
finds it tender, moving through
the streets below, looking this way and that,
past all the gray dressed days,
moments dancing in red and me
still searching, needing,
waiting for the moment you arrive.

The River Princess

If you want her, want her as the river would,
call her in with cackles and whispers,
a whole mouth of secrets.
Carve her name on the banks,
tell her to come and see.
Let her moment be unstable,
balanced on such a brink as she is.

Take her then, white and pliant as a bride,
through all your long shadows,
past the small places where she could have lived
and died having never had a story.
Carry her along your beautiful miles
and she will weave bouquets of leaves and twine,
and she shall be a mystery, a memory,
immortal in the minds of those who say
they knew her once upon a time.

Letters to You in Winter

Weeks ago now, I wrote
about how the days would get longer,
the worst remaining a few miles back
even as January blows between us
like a black-iced road, straight,
impenetrable. I am standing by it
and my pretension for the instant
is that I know you well enough to know
that somewhere the ice is breaking,
you are heading for summer
in your oldest shoes, dreaming of driving
a series of convertible moments,
a colored line to the coast, to the tarrying boats.

I, myself, can't get past the echoing trains,
can't take my eyes off the birds
of the air in their coats of metal and flesh.
I want you to know that I have wished
nearly enough to make their trek mine,
have drawn closer to you in time, my friend,
to the warm hour when we are
both together and alone.

Mourning Midas

Midas, have you ever seen October dressed
in morning, just west of the great divide?
The air grows light and easy here, hanging
in the balance of sunbeams and chill,
not flavored of afternoon familiarity, no dung
or tumbleweeds this time. Just aspen gold
at rest on blankets of evergreen. Breathe
deep, my darling, you can smell the leaves.

And what is it you recall of our summer days?
That you left your fingerprints upon my skin,
the shade of my hair across your face
in some oddly shared dream? You say your city
is different now, it no longer respects your barriers.
It breaks down your connectivity, rushes you. You say
you cannot write in such a place. Midas,
I am statue still and golden like October.
I've stored my tears in tiny bottles
for you to drink and live again.

And if my autumn offerings are not the awakening
you seek, I shall become a pastel flock of paper swans
floating on Lake Biwa in the spring.
The white diamonds of Everest's cap.
A sand hued snake in the middle of the Sahara,
jambalaya in New Orleans. Anything you need, love,
just let me see the touch of your words upon a world
left shimmering, trembling by you as I have been.

Past the Cul de Sac

When you say there's a road I should be on,
I am already running barefoot, wishing
not for another mile, but another field,
just one damn sunset that doesn't begin with the end,
another childlike summer and you
more than a small flower on the side
that I can be only so much of, a kiss print
on the tip of every petal in a shade as foreign to nature
as my name to the sky and I can only hope
it's enough a sign so that when your roots grow
wings and you fly, you'll find me
on the corner of Ash and Night, waiting for you
as I have always waited. This is my life.

Consider

Consider me, the hideaway queen,
the one afraid of the whole world watching.
Having taken to my nest,
safely buried my head, I can still hear you
speak of the time when you ventured high,
how the earth wobbled small beneath you,
that you jumped if for nothing but simply
to transcend the fear. You say you'd do it again.

Consider this, me glancing up,
grinning at the thought. I, too, have climbed
to the height of everything so I can give you
something to remember, how the air is clear up here,
the sky a single tremor away,
how this is the juncture in which to be alive,
tensed in such a born-with want,
a golden truth, impossible to hold.

Consider the day, that I'll find myself
flying through it, searching for you in a crowd
of a thousand, all those faces looking up
in earnest for someone to believe in.
And maybe they'll smile when I write for them,
but you'll still be the only one
who truly knows where the words come from.
Consider that, the next time you jump.

Once Green

After all, what could be said of the leaves
we crush underfoot but that we remember them

as we remember ourselves: part of something,
two children in the park, burdening each other

with our play, thoughts of winter to come;
that we shall remain as they: perennially young,

growing mornings from whispers, how long
these arms that reach upwards, elevation

by inches as we shine with the wanting
to leap, to dance on air and – in our own time –

to risk a sidewalk kiss in the middle of someday,
regardless of the consequences.

The Arrogance of Two

Let's just be poets then,
in skins that don't bruise so easily.
You can wear your mad hat,
I shall don my dress of confession.

Let's pretend the world only sees us
as invisible; that is, for all they know
there are simply scraps of paper,
poems that write themselves

and maybe we are wintering
on a beach in Tahiti, washing our old souls
in that far sea or perhaps we are as near
as the edge of the nearest high bridge,

watching them in their problem suits,
all the words they don't understand,
how thought itself becomes an ocean so big
that they have forgotten to look for us.

Abell 2218

Day has grown tired already,
is the sigh that follows farewell
and the angels are weeping again.
Damn rain, slipping
to soil like nails to skin,
digging a grave
that only holds them
until they can make their escape
to rivulets, puddles,
drops of silver light
leading nowhere
beyond this tiny circle
of time, this river of regret
that appears to the sky
as little more
than a backseat blur
from a Buick doing sixty
down an endless highway,
running from something
that never fades - a galaxy
light years away,
someone on the radio
who sounds a lot like you:
Are we there yet?

I study the instant,
this glittering diamond,
this blushing salt mine of mine
and I wonder who can hold this sea, not I,
and why you didn't call me your angel

when the instant passed me by.
Just another fortune lost
in the desert between here and there
and I have ripped away the rearview,
pressed the pedal to the floor.

I am still pretending I'll be home before dark.

The Last Butterfly

It is a siren,
this unfettered urge of yours to sing,
as though just born this morning
and already past the milk of things,
having glimpsed the future yesterday,
returned and returned again.

Still, all I know is this little life,
this certain order of things: I breathe, I fly,
I live at the edge of perdition.
And you, you are so beautiful this morning,
your golden fingers through the branches
as if reaching

is a reason for being, as though
my capture could make you a god
and I wonder how well you know yourself,
if you see the particular way
you've arranged the clouds,
what part of tomorrow you will remember

forever: if it is I,
drunk on the colors of you,
drowning in your oil rainbow,
or how gently sweetness passes itself,
its wings spread out like arms,
like a cross. Tomorrow,
I shall sing with you
for I have no other way to die.

*Part Three:
Confined by Need*

Solitary Confinement

Free, somewhere,
of the day's inscrutable silence,
a shadow floats the edge
of the tiles, the wall, converses
with your heart in flutters and leaps.

You are reading by lamplight, alone
but not lonely for I am with you,
have come when you called,
so less in matter than thought.
In a swell of unused energy,
in your thirsty want for pretty things,

I am with you.

What is Effortless

or urgent. Or only lost in the little thoughts of finding you in a nearish dark, in a haze so hot as to be anything but a dream. You here, in the bracken between that which is and is unseen, in the way I have taken the word aubade and tied it around the letters of your name until all that is left is what can be said in a single breath:

I am...

I am, and the tremble begins. I am, and the air becomes electric, the day insistent on fading away but I have not yet become it, the day, pressed as fruit to your lips, soft on your skin, I have not and so the breath must come again:

I am...

I am, and a morning storm can hold a thousand hues. I am, and only I can say which way this song will end: *alive... awake... aubade...* I am away with my little thoughts of you, here in this nearish dawn of what I want and want to become, tied to the tides of each breathless breath, I am, I am...

No Words for Summer's End

There is no sleep for certain storms, nothing to keep you from watching the window, seeing me outside, waiting to be pulled through, warmed beneath you, comforted. Need is merely a hard rain, you say, and there is a hole in the ceiling. We cannot escape.

I fear how you search for paradise, that you believe I have swallowed it, have hidden it inside my skin; that the banks of me may not be enough to hold the grief when you find that you cannot find it, that I am not heaven's womb after all. I am only a woman.

Still, there is strength in sweetness, grace in pretending that we have yet to know each other, that my fingerprints are not already burned on this glasslike desire to kneel before you, to have you honor my reverence with your own.

Tonight, we are but hours, sweetheart, nothing more than ticks of the clock, a secret closet in a world of rooms; only a candle, a small and burning light so bright that there are no words for it, no words at all.

Shaped by this Need

I.

I am trying to tell you how it is for us,
in a way that makes your soul sing
even as the mind fights it, I am speaking
of your soul as if it was a universe, a city,
the particular way you arrange your hands
and perhaps it is in them, your hands,
that the answer rests. When you asked me why
I would end my poems with a short note:
should you wish to read them,
it was your hands I was thinking of,
how different they are, how bound
to the process of shaping.
There is creation in your hands but mine
are so very small, are wind spent birds, fluttering
this way or that, stroking the beautiful but never
enough. They drown in the kitchen sink,
these hands, in a froth of snow
when the morning is too cold for flying.

II.

If you could, for once,
hold this soap of my soul,
touch its transient warmth,
could smell the scent of me,
it would still not be me but merely an echo of I,
a thin drift, a feathering for the moment,

a gift: *should you wish to claim it.*
And once claimed, I can only dream the ways
you would shape me beneath your weight, carve
a place to bury your face, to bury your secrets,
to bury the scar of us. If I remember anything,
I shall remember this: I can neither remain
a gift or a drift, a moment is but a path
to something for once far greater
than you or I alone could ever know.

III.

Even from your city, you have felt
the rise and fall of my laughter, my fear;
the landscape of breath that carries me
from season to season. You know
these dreams, my news reports have been
delivered to your door with unabashed regularity
as I am shaped by this need to have you know me,
to be that gutter fed trickle, signs of a neighbor
who hand washes the sidewalk even in winter
so that, when water begins to flow uphill,
you will come, will find this place,
will find me beautiful.

IV.

Whatever happens to us will happen
on separate sheets, different chapters, will be
snowflakes on far flung blood fields,
 the only common characteristic

being that which defines us: war
with ourselves, our own skins,
our own limitations. What time is granted
is granted unrequited, love,
presses itself into a downtown bus,
into all the forgotten spaces, you at one end
and I at another, afforded only so many glances,
for to look too often or too hard would be to regret
our very lives, how they are sewn
to this patchwork distantly, carelessly, our colors
matched more to those who were born to find us
than those we were born searching for.

When Clicking Heels Offer No Escape
(Dorothy Says to the Wizard)

Mix me up
a ruby red river
to drown the bleach
bleeding from these white
washed walls. Speak
in tones of passionate
pink, bottomless blue.

Turn me on
to neutral: yellow brick shades
of winter's morning sky. Shake
from me the colorless
stare until my teeth rattle,
until I make it past
the pale scream.

Take me
by the wrists, let your fingers
do the jagged shadow walk
on the echo of the blade;
that black, black memory,
the way it used to be. Say it's over
now, take me home

somewhere over the rainbow...

You First

If someone would have told us
you were going to don your cardboard armor,
saddle up the broom, ride in
at the closing strains of my happily ever after;
that we'd hide in the woods each morning,
make Indian burns on our vulnerabilities;
that love only had to be claimed
by the one who cried uncle,
I would have replied as if it was a question:
False.

And if they would have told us later
that we would spin the bottle broken;
spend months discovering the heart
and that it made a good game piece
for chicken; that the cop and the robber
would both find themselves at the edge of the cliff
when the world yelled double dare,
you would have narrowed your eyes, smiled,
would have turned to me and said:
You first.

Some Days

At dawn it dawns again:
all those fierce and hungry deaths,
signs of fall: a bruise on her knee,
dead leaves, the way you fade
in the light. By noon, she will be buried
in pity and cigarettes, will have wallowed
for hours by the washing machine,
pretending that spinning space is womb,
small comfort from the stain of her life

and only then will she come to you
on a well worn path, nearly complete
in her need, nearly hoping
you'll walk away this time, leave her
to scream alone, but this time
you simply take the ribboned thoughts
of her, gather the scattered colors,
hold them tight in the hollow of your arms.
And all the while, she is still so afraid

that the dream is too far to reach,
that there is no white island
called someday, no one to save her, and you
don't know any more than all the times before,
no less than you'll know tomorrow
but still you take her face in your hands,
tell her to look, look harder. And only then
do you walk away, leave her with twilight, a kiss,
and some days faith rises again, just like this.

Alive

You've seen it before but never in morning:
the pink tinged ridge, a canyon in dawning,
a river of pulse beneath it,
alive even as she dies in her dreaming, alive
and seemingly speaking. Listen.

This is the story not categorized, alphabetized,
the title you'll never see alongside Broken
Mickey Mouse Ring, Age 5, or Bicycle Accident,
Second Grade, these are the uncharted waters
of her and you try to imagine it, the way

it tells you in that still-girl voice,
I didn't think I had a choice, and you can see it:
that rage red stain; in truth,
you could always see it
reflected in her eyes, her silence and you know

how later is, that now you'll start to see
it in every black winged fledgling girl
in every curb shadow and you'll be thinking
my god, who touched her, who made her
hide in a corner, pick up a razor,

how thick was the boulder they rolled
before her, that they never heard her words?
My God, you think, this glorious day
almost never happened at all and all
you really want is to stop thinking about it,

to start the morning over, somewhere else
on that landscape of her, all you really want
is the person you think she is,
without all the yesterdays and you know
how yesterday is, that haunting voice never shuts up

unless your hand is over it,
so you grasp her wrist, awaken her
with a kiss, but you cannot forget
the river that turns, burns beneath your fingers,
silent but alive. Oh, still so alive.

But She Wrote Anyway

as if no one had ever written
a letter to the ocean before,
the prayer of it so blurred
that nothing remained but love
and a name, a salt scented kiss
caught in the post script.

as if it rained in your city today
and you laughed like a child,
your feet buried deep in the grass
and you never felt so clean
as you did when you were hoping
she would write you just like that.

I Still Need You

I am trying to calm the starved girl
who lives inside of me, who beats
upon the windows of memory, rattles
the cage bars of my chest, but she needs
a song of summer things, needs me to sing
her back to sleep and all I can think

is that you're gone again, darling, faded
to little more than a shimmer, and sometimes
you remind me so much of her, but you don't
even know that girl, have only seen her
shadow when I am hiding, writing a blackness
you can't understand and I need you

to touch me, to tell me to remember
that the girl is long dead, hold my hands
so I won't dig up her grave, so I won't give her
my breath again and again. I need you to know
that she was stronger than they said and you said
I am stronger than I think, but I still need you

to remind me to sing for myself this time.

Unfinished Symphony

Now when she watches from the bridge,
it is only your hands she sees, stirring
the yellows, the greens, and how reluctantly
you turn from her face, focus on trees
that shall trap her in your forever autumn.

Even unseen, the world already knows her as Symphony,
has fallen in love and nearly silent with their awe
of you. These days, everyone waits to call you maestro,
reverence painted on their cheeks as if with your brush.

And it's been a year since you saw her there,
watching you paint, and later in black velvet dreams,
where it was you who became complete
in the canvas of her, trying to remember
if her eyes were brown or green.

It was you who shook your head that day – *no* –
when she said the name of another: Midas;
who learned from her mistake what it feels like to want
to be somebody else, to begin each breath with if only.

Now all you can do is offer her image
to a world gone golden, a world that pines for the words:
I understand. It was she who gave herself
to your ascent, who still holds that perfect moment
in the way you drew her hands.

When everything changed, she knew you first.

Part Four:
Reasons, Meanings

She Whispered to the Moon

And she said, there is splendor
in the surrender, glory in black satin
wrapping all those bright and tiny breaths.

Beautiful, the burden of being
a particle of dream, created of dust and ash
and want, swallowed whole and hungry.

And she said, there is bidding
in the forbidden, ransoms made
for the giving, kisses meant to be stolen.

Beautiful, the burning of being
swept to the center of it all, taken
in as nourishment, cast out as embers.

And he replied, I give you back
in pieces, petals of night-blooming flowers,
wild wishes, miracles too delicate for day.

In everything I am, I give you back.

Lily, You Said

As though title alone
could capture a girl, plant her
warm in the palm of your hands,

could make her feel
the sweet stroke of rain,
all the beautiful aches
the world knows well

but cannot explain, the way
summer lasts an instant,
is a series of small deaths,
a diamond in the distance.

And I can feel you now,
moving through the fields,
coming nearer in your measure

of moments, months,
always just out of reach
but I am still reaching,

growing tall with want,
drunk on sky, even now I
can feel you like the liquid slip,

sun on my skin,
my name on your lips. Lily,
Lily, you said.

What He Did

It's not as if he pushed the pen into her hand,
leaned forward with all the grim clenched
properties of force, placed a contract before her
with a hundred dotted lines. Actually,

he kept his distance, gestured softly
to a world between them of unmarked walls,
roadways that bore no signs, only said
this is ours and then watched as she moved

beyond the borders, climbed high a silent bridge,
dropping pages as she went, only watched
as the city began to speak
about the elusive you, the mysterious him,

only watched until she, herself, was little more
than a bright and heavenly dot,
taking a pen from her pocket to scribble
two names across the sky. That's what he did.

The Greatest Fear

is silence. That, having not dreamt
of drowning this time, I would rise
without trembling or that bone-deep need
for saving; would rise without planning
all possible escapes in case this day should burn;

without anyone to tell me
whose life this is, how it must be spent; without
anyone to let me give up. I would rise anyway
in silence, having thrown away that tattered suitcase
of myself, still remembering what was inside,
those syllables of doubt all folded and pressed;
remembering how I looked in that melancholy dress
when I said that dying was pretty,
how I practiced it for years; still remembering
that the reason I hung on so long is silence.

That, having ventured this far and afraid,
I might see you but you wouldn't know my name;
I might see you, your smile so sweet, so blank,
and you would be kind to a stranger
who swears she knows you,
gentle in the sidestep; I might see you,
but you would walk on in silence.

Speaking of Today

Today is a girl in second hand
shoes, yarn-tied hair and a mood

that is quite frightful. It would be enough
for you to let her pass by, a blip

on the radar, a turning of a page,
a sentence that starts again

with "I can't remember..."
It would be enough to forget but you

just keep holding on, want her to live
right this instant, every inching stroke

of the moment. You want to ponder
that little life, roll it on your tongue,

deem it lacking in salt. You want sunshine
in the morning, sex in the afternoon, a dream

of you in the winding down. You just keep
holding on, even as she is twisting, slipping

from your grasp. And she never asked
to be so changed, so strangely loved.

No, she never asked.

And Then, She Opens Her Eyes

"Is it you, my prince?" said she to him. "You have waited a long while." – Sleeping Beauty

We have not yet reached the ocean,
not felt salt burrowing in the creases
of clasped palms or shivered
whispers spraying our flesh
like secrets. I am tugged
by you, by wind, urging me closer
to promise, benediction.

We are still moving through forests,
dropping off faces of rocks like tears,
like wedding rice. I am tossing
through waves of fear, frayed
hems, skin-scrapes. The clasp
of my suitcase has come undone, history
is scattered. Hurry, you say.

We keep covering the same ground,
always waiting for the symphony,
the ballet. You tell me this is sunrise,
an unblemished page. I am turning
in tales of lost things, longing to hold
tight to old treasures. Still
you are pulling me forward.

We lose record of time, instants are eternal
gateways between was and will
be, a break in the trees. You reach

the end an instant before me. I am tangled
in roots, wrapped still
in night. You are morning: transcendence,
light. Stirring, you are stirring me
from a hundred years' sleep with kisses, and the sea.

Another Autumn

In spite of tomorrow, or maybe
because of it, I find myself
turning to last year, its bumper crop leaves
and other scraped away things
I swore I would forget. I was
the one with the angry pose, the old
my mother hates me stance. There was
a single time I never answered you,
and you said: what is it, girl,
you have not learned to accept?

These days, I am more wisp
than whisper, a bit of ash,
a black cat. I unfold in the darkness,
not yet willing to call it my own,
to claim its flip side light,
that I am - have always been -
a candle burning.

What is it you told me? - A year
is such a small bit of time.
This time, I am - have always been -
set to press myself to your shadow,
your mind, to that one safe place
outside myself. But you
have mirrored the hallways,
hold a handful of snapshots,
my very best words. You
are still so beautiful,

even in my small reflection, even
as I learn to answer the question:

In spite of tomorrow, or maybe
because of it, I find myself...

Reconciliation

I, still so much
a child in your hands,
cheeks kissed
as if by winter,
breath labored first
from running away
and later, running to.

You, born to make me
a flame, to reckon
my name with the dust
of stars. There are
no words between us
that do not sizzle,
spark; no songs to which

we have not danced.

You Had Your Reasons

"And a thing which is led is led because one leads it, and a thing which is seen is so because one sees it?"
– Socrates

Because that virtue
was still so locked inside you,
so hidden beneath the black ceilings
of their rituals, between the walls of their piety
that you dreamt a wind with wings,
a fluttering flood of a hundred hues;

Because some thirsted for blues, ribboned
a path to the ocean and became then
the sacrificial slivers, the fattened rivers;
Because some gazed their green reflection,
their recollected youth and grew, themselves,
into the very truth of seasons;

Because some grasped bits of silver, gold,
and from it, the hunger for quest,
the act of saving, of handing down;
Because some envisioned violet
and therefore learned the heady scent of lust,
the intoxicating wilderness of woman;

Because that last butterfly was the one
you might have loved in spite of reason
and beyond all realm of possibility;
Because she lingered on your moistened fingers,
drank your velvet whispers, and when you said:

I am ready, she believed;

Because she was such a brilliant red,
the remaining guardsmen could only see
the stain of your life, their own self-conviction
and so they bitterly wept, never hearing
the lilt of your final breath;
never knowing how far it carried her.

The Meaning of This

If I am only a whisper, let me be the whisper of morning, thread of a dream, cord of a newborn day. Let me be the instant the traffic stills, a birdsong beyond the walls of the highrise, the sun glinting off the window's edge.

If you are only a road, be the one to carry me through hours, the continuous line beside me, be the graffiti on the water tower that says above all else, *hope*, with a year beside it, let me know that time doesn't matter, the line never breaks.

If we are nothing but pieces, let us be pieces of summer, shells on opposite beaches, holding all the light the world has ever known in the smooth cups of our hands. Let us hide in the sand until we find ourselves again. Let it be this simple.

Let it be.

Nearly Home

and when you rise in the dreary
damp of morning, dawn the day
in all its disguises, hide her little life
in your pocket, the loose change
of it like small and simple rhymes
to your every weighted step.

Take her to the fountain, and remember
this: the silver splash
that fills you with wishes to spend her
wisely, like diamonds or dimes, glimmering
deep in a sea of need, that you would slip
softly to shadows, watch the half-starved
beggars move in, squabbling over her
as geese for crumbs,

and you would neglect your own hunger
just to see them flying, carrying her words
to the city below, where the people go
to pray for rain. You can almost feel it
now: her blind white freefall through all
the layers of light, how she has never been
so free, so nearly home on the cheeks
of a million strangers, yes, so nearly home.

Acknowledgments

Cover art © 2005 by Mitchell Miller,
used with permission.

Shotgun previously published in *The Paumanok Review*; Mourning Midas previously published in *The Rose and Thorn*; Once Green previously published in *Softblow*; Shaped by This Need previously published in *Poems Niederngasse*; You First previously published in *Poetry Super Highway*; Alive, third place winner at IBPC, Nov. 2004, previously published in *The Paumanok Review*; Abell 2218 previously published in *Wicked Alice*; Lily, You Said previously published in *Softblow*; And Then, She Opens Her Eyes previously published in *The Pedestal Magazine*; Reconciliation previously published in *Softblow*.

Printed in the United States
40050LVS00009B/197